D1223615

Rocky Mountain National Park

by Lisa M. Herrington

Content Consultant
Nanci R. Vargus, Ed.D.
Professor Emeritus, University of Indianapolis

Reading Consultant
Jeanne M. Clidas, Ph.D.
Reading Specialist

Children's Press®
An Imprint of Scholastic Inc.

Library of Congress Cataloging-in-Publication Data
Names: Herrington, Lisa M., author.
Title: Rocky Mountain National Park/by Lisa M. Herrington.
Description: New York, NY: Children's Press, an imprint of Scholastic Inc., 2018. |
Series: Rookie national parks | Includes index.
Identifiers: LCCN 2016055220| ISBN 9780531233337 (library binding) |
ISBN 9780531239056 (paperback)
Subjects: LCSH: Rocky Mountain National Park (Colo.)—Juvenile literature. |
Rocky Mountains—Juvenile literature.
Classification: LCC F782.R59 H47 2018 | DDC 978.8/69—dc23
LC record available at https://lccn.loc.gov/2016055220

Produced by Spooky Cheetah Press
Design: Judith Christ-Lafond/Joan Michael

Published in 2018 by Children's Press, an imprint of Scholastic Inc., 557 Broadway,
New York, NY 10012.

Printed in China 62

1 2 3 4 5 6 7 8 9 10 R 27 26 25 24 23 22 21 20 19 18

Photographs ©: cover: Jon Arnold Images Ltd/Alamy Images; back cover:
imageBROKER/Superstock, Inc.; 1-2: PCRex/Shutterstock; 3: Mike Berenson/Colorado
Captures/Getty Images; 4-5: Wayne Boland/Getty Images; 6-7: RondaKimbrow/
iStockphoto; 8-9: milehightraveler/iStockphoto; 10-11: Ethan Welty/Getty Images;
12-13: dancestrokes/iStockphoto; 14: kellyvandellen/Getty Images; 15: unclegene/
iStockphoto; 16-17: MRaust/iStockphoto; 18-19: Sandra Leidholdt/Getty Images; 20-
21 background: Sumio Harada/Minden Pictures; 21 top inset: W. Perry Conway/age
fotostock; 21 bottom inset: Education Images/UIG/Getty Images; 22-23 background:
NetaDegany/iStockphoto; 23 top inset: James Frank Stock Connection Worldwide/
Newscom; 23 bottom inset: epicurean/iStockphoto; 24-25: Deddeda/Getty Images;
26-30 background: DavidMSchrader/iStockphoto; 26 top left: Sloot/iStockphoto; 26
top center: Musat Christian/Dreamstime; 26 top right: Joel Sartore/Getty Images; 26
bottom left: KenCanning/iStockphoto; 26 bottom center: DEA/C.DANI/I.JESKE/Getty
Images; 26 bottom right: GlobalP/iStockphoto; 27 top left: Josef Pittner/Shutterstock;
27 top right: Sumio Harada/Minden Pictures; 27 bottom left: Isselee/Dreamstime; 27
bottom center: DCorn/iStockphoto; 27 bottom right: Jeff R Clow/Getty Images; 30
top left: Gunter Marx Photography/Getty Images; 30 bottom left: bgfoto/iStockphoto;
30 top right: McPHOTO/age fotostock; 30 bottom right: Mark Chappell/age
fotostock; 30 top left inset: Kellie Eldridge/Dreamstime; 30 top right inset: srekapi/
iStockphoto; 31 top: tjwvandongen/iStockphoto; 31 center top: Yva Momatiuk and
John Eastcott/Minden Pictures; 31 center bottom: axnjax/Getty Images; 31 bottom:
John Lemker/age fotostock; 32: Jon Arnold Images Ltd/Alamy Images.

Maps by Jim McMahon.

Table of Contents

Introduction

I am Ranger
Red Fox, your tour guide.
Are you ready for an amazing
adventure in Rocky?

Welcome to Rocky Mountain National Park!

"Rocky" was made a **national park** in 1915. People visit parks like this one to explore nature.

Rocky Mountain National Park is named for the mountain range that runs through it. It is located in Colorado.

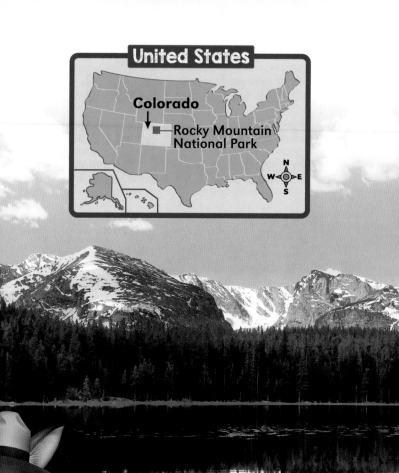

United States

Colorado

Rocky Mountain
National Park

N
W E
S

About three
million people visit
Rocky each year.

This park has it all. You may see rugged cliffs and snowcapped mountains. There are evergreen forests and clear lakes. Many plants and animals live here, too.

Rocky spans 415 square miles (1,075 square kilometers). That is about six times as large as Washington, D.C.

This is Andrews Glacier. It is one of several small glaciers left in the park today.

It is a 5-mile (8-kilometer) hike to this glacier. Whew! I'm tired!

Chapter 1

Mighty Mountains

The park is part of the Rocky Mountains. This western mountain range runs all the way to Canada.

Long ago, glaciers helped shape the park. As these huge pieces of ice slowly melted, they left behind massive mountains. They also carved out **valleys** between the mountains.

Some of the highest mountains in the United States are found in the park. It has 78 **peaks** that are more than 2 miles (3 kilometers) high! Many are covered with snow year-round.

This is the place to go if you want to feel on top of the world!

At 14,259 feet (4,346 meters), Longs Peak is the park's tallest mountain.

About one-third of the park is above the tree line. That is where trees stop growing.

Chapter 2

A Land of Extremes

Brrr! The top of the park is very cold and windy. You will find mountain **tundra** here. That is land where it is too cold for trees to grow. Only small plants and grasses grow.

Melting snow turns into rushing water at Alberta Falls.

As you move down the mountain, the landscape changes. Trees grow on the slopes below the tundra. They include pine, aspen, and blue spruce trees.

Streams flow over some mountain cliffs into wild waterfalls. There are also many lakes and rivers.

Evergreens keep their needlelike leaves year-round.

Douglas fir

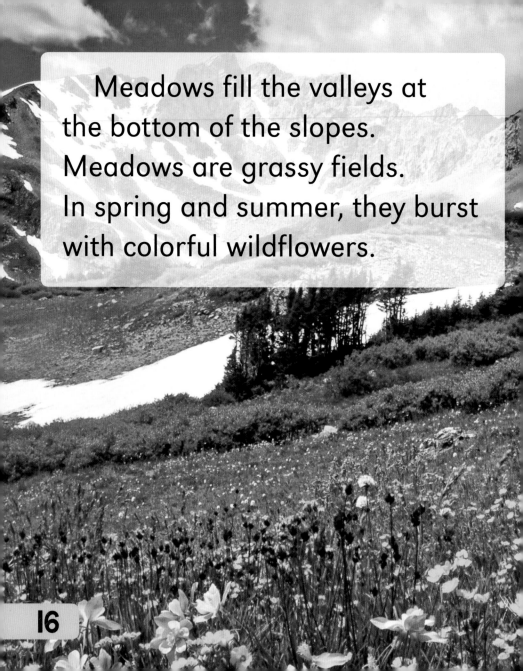

Meadows fill the valleys at the bottom of the slopes. Meadows are grassy fields. In spring and summer, they burst with colorful wildflowers.

Hundreds of types of flowering plants grow in the park.

Chapter 3

Amazing Animals

When you visit the park, bring your binoculars! Rocky is famous for its large animals. Bighorn sheep cling to rocky ledges. Elk, mule deer, and moose graze in the valley.

About 350 bighorn sheep live in the park.

Yellow-bellied marmots look for plants to eat on the mountainside.

Many small animals are found here, too. They include chipmunks and furry, squirrel-like marmots. Beavers live near rivers. Eagles and falcons soar high above. More than 140 kinds of beautiful butterflies flutter through the meadows.

bald eagle

painted lady butterfly

Chapter 4

A Park for All Seasons

There are lots of ways to see the park. One way is by car. Trail Ridge Road rises into the tundra. No other continuous paved road in the U.S. will take you as high.

You can explore on foot, too. Some people climb the towering mountains. They hike tough trails. Others fish, ride horses, and camp.

Some trails are perfect for a horseback ride.

Experienced rock climbers find big challenges at Rocky.

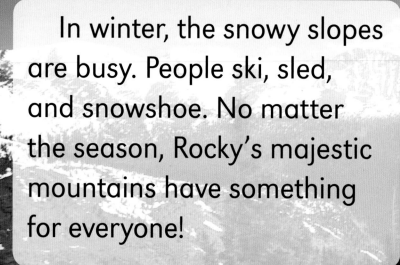

In winter, the snowy slopes are busy. People ski, sled, and snowshoe. No matter the season, Rocky's majestic mountains have something for everyone!

Imagine you could visit Rocky. What would you do there?

24

These are just some of the incredible animals that make their home in Rocky.

painted lady butterfly

beaver

boreal toad

bighorn sheep

yellow-bellied marmot

mountain lion

Wildlife by the Numbers
The park is home to about...

270 types of birds   **67** types of mammals

The bighorn sheep is the symbol of Rocky Mountain National Park.

elk

pika

bald eagle

mule deer

moose

6 types of reptiles and amphibians

11 types of fish

Where Is Ranger Red Fox?

Oh no! Ranger Red Fox has lost his way in the park. But you can help. Use the map and the clues below to find him.

1. Ranger Red Fox got lost on a hiking trail near Trio Falls.

2. He ran north and stumbled upon Bear Lake.

3. Next, he headed southwest and found an ancient glacier.

4. Finally, he hiked southeast. He ended up near this towering mountain.

Help! Can you find me?

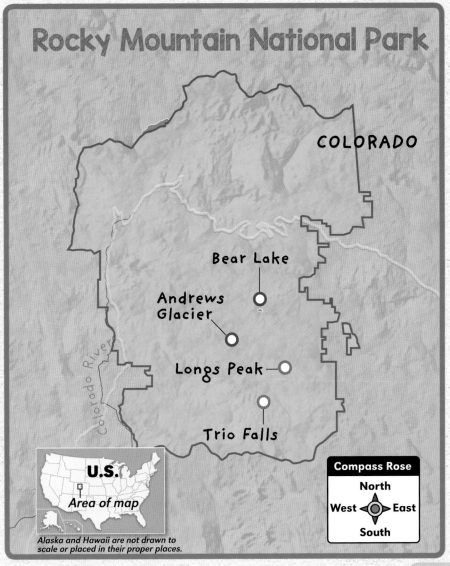

Rocky Mountain National Park

COLORADO

Bear Lake

Andrews
Glacier

Longs Peak

Trio Falls

Colorado River

U.S.
Area of map

Alaska and Hawaii are not drawn to
scale or placed in their proper places.

Compass Rose

North

West ◆ East

South

Can you guess which leaf belongs to which tree in Rocky? Read the clues to help you.

A.

1. Colorado blue spruce
Clue: This tree gets its name from its silver-blue needles.

2. Lodgepole pine
Clue: This tree has long, thin needles that come in bundles of two.

3. Quaking aspen
Clue: This tree's round leaves turn red, orange, and yellow in fall.

B.

4. Douglas fir
Clue: This tree has short, thin needles. Narrow cones hang from its branches.

D.

C.

Answers: 1. D, 2. A, 3. C, 4. B

Glossary

national park (**nash**-uh-nuhl pahrk): area where the land and its animals are protected by the U.S. government

peaks (**peeks**): pointed tops of mountains

tundra (**tuhn**-druh): cold area of land where no trees grow and the soil beneath the surface is always frozen

valleys (**val**-eez): areas of low ground between two hills or mountains, usually containing a river

Index

Facts for Now

Visit this Scholastic Web site for more information
on Rocky Mountain National Park:
www.factsfornow.scholastic.com
Enter the keywords **Rocky Mountain**

About the Author

Lisa M. Herrington has written many books for kids. She loves exploring our country's beautiful national parks. Lisa lives in Connecticut with her husband and daughter.